What Time Is It?

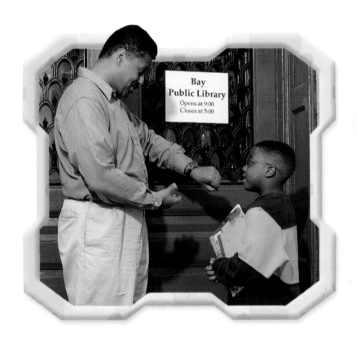

Maggie Bridger

Sadlier-Oxford
A Division of William H. Sadlier, Inc.

Contents

What time is it? Look at
a clock to find out.

Look at this clock. The number 7 tells the hour. The number 30 tells the minutes.

What time is it?

It's 7:30. Time to get ready for school!

Look at this clock. The hour hand is pointing to 11. The minute hand is pointing to 12.

What time is it?

It's 11:00. Time for a snack!

8

Look at this clock. The hour hand is between 3 and 4. The minute hand is pointing to 6.

What time is it?

It's 3:30. Time for kickball!

Sometimes it's hard to keep track of time.

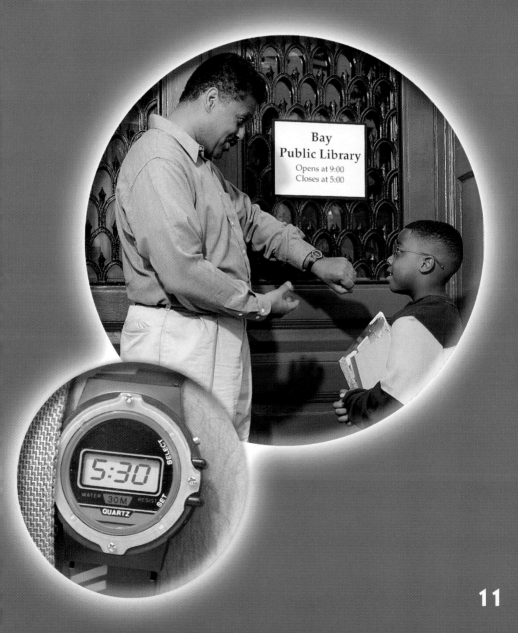

A schedule can help.

Time	Activity
3:30	kickball
4:30	library
5:30	supper
8:00	bedtime

Look at the clock. Now look back at the schedule. What time is it?

It's 8:00. Time to turn out the light!

Good night!

Make a Clock

What You Need:

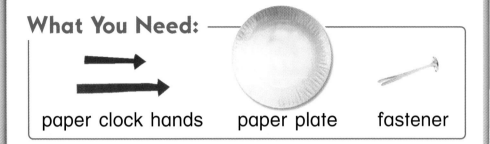

paper clock hands   paper plate   fastener

What You Do:

1. Write the numbers 1 to 12 around the plate. Make it look like a clock face.

2. Use a pencil to make a small hole in the middle of the plate.

3. Fasten the hands to the clock.

4. Move the hands to show a time to the hour or half hour. Ask a partner to draw the clock and to write the time.

Index